"Dear Bud"
V-Mail Stories from WWII

Lt. Col. Isadore "Sparky" Spark, M.D.

Illustrations by Michelle Seigei Spark
Introduction & Afterword by Ronald Spark, M.D.

ISBN 9798263686802
Copyright ©2025 by Ronald Spark, M.D.

INTRODUCTION

This book is a collection of letters written by a father "Sparky" to his young son, "Bud." That little boy was me! My father was sent overseas to Europe by the U.S. Army during WWII to serve as a doctor. He'd had to leave my mother and me to serve his country, even though I was only three years old. So, these letters were an important link — in fact the only link — between us from 1944-45.

Because I was so young, and could not possibly understand what Sparky was experiencing, my father did not write about his day-to-day life in the Army in England and France. (I don't think he could have said much anyway, because of wartime censorship!) Instead, my father wrote delightful tales about imaginary characters including a friendly stove and a talking jeep. Sparky wrote to me as if we were there together at bedtime — me listening and him telling the story. As you will see, he was a marvelous storyteller.

These letters are special for another reason. They were what was called "V-Mail" or Victory Mail. V-Mail was an almost magical way of sending letters from men stationed overseas to their families "state side" in the USA. The way it worked was — tiny photos or "microfilms" were taken of all the mail. Hundreds of letters could miraculously be sent on one small roll of film. Once the microfilm reached America, the letters were reprinted full size and sent on their way.

Believe it or not, these letters were forgotten for many years. I was very excited when, as an adult, I rediscovered them. I showed them to my father but to my surprise, he didn't want to look at them again. I think his time serving in the war, and being separated from his family, was perhaps one of the most painful things that happened to him. He simply did not want to revisit those memories. For me though, these stories will always be something wonderful, showing my father's caring, thoughtfulness and love for me.

Thanks to the efforts of my sister Michelle, my daughter Marie and my granddaughter Celeste, I am now able to share these stories with you. I hope you enjoy them!

Ronald Spark, M.D.

P.S.: You may be wondering why my father chose to call me "Bud." Well, he explained this to me in a letter: "... a bud is intriguing in its possibilities. It looks fine and promises to grow beautiful and handsome. It needs good care now for the future it may have. It opens its face to the world when things are warm and bright."

Geradline Spark, Isadore "Sparky" Spark and Bud 1942

January 2, 1944

Dear Bud –

A funny thing happened today. A soldier brought in a lot of letters, and in the pile of letters, we heard "Woof woof." Everyone was surprised because we never received letters before that said "Woof woof." So we

looked and looked. And then we found one letter that was making all the noise. "Woof woof woof," it said. I picked it up and saw it was for me, and that my Bud had sent it. Then I listened more and heard:

"Woof woof. Let me out!" So I opened the letter and there was your Puppy Dog!

Puppy Dog was very tired because he had had a long trip. "Woof woof," he said. I fed him and put him to bed. And he said, "Woof woof. Goodnight." I was very pleased to get him. He wished me a happy birthday and said, "Woof Woof, Bud sent me." I was glad my boy was so kind to his daddy. I knew you wanted me to let Puppy Dog run and play. We let him run and he went up to old Buttons the Bulldog and said "Woof woof" and Buttons said, "Grr, Grr." They were friends from then on. Now Puppy Dog lives with Buttons the Bulldog and is happy.

Isn't that fine, Bud?

Sparky

June 30, 1944

Dear Bud –

Do you know what I saw today? I saw a big black and white Momma Dog. She was barking "Bow wow" and running and looking around. What do you think she was looking for? I watched to see if I could find out. Very soon I heard "Yip yip yip" coming from behind a tree, and then a teeny tiny, black and white Little Puppy Dog scampered out wagging his tail. They stood there and barked at each other.

Momma Dog said "Bow wow - you come here and eat this nice bone." Little Puppy Dog said, "Yip, yip, Momma. I'd rather have a nice run through the woods." So, Momma Dog picked up Little Puppy Dog, carried him in her mouth, and put him down in front of the bone, because she wanted him to eat his supper. "Bow wow," said Momma Dog, "If you don't eat now, I'll eat it myself and then you'll be hungry." "Yip, yip," said Little Puppy Dog, "Okay Momma, I don't want to be hungry, because when I'm hungry I can't sleep." "Bow Wow," said Momma Dog. "Well, go ahead and eat the bone."

So the Little Puppy Dog sat down and was very quiet because he is a good Little Puppy Dog, and he ate the bone all up. "Yip, yip," said he. "That was good, Yum yum." "Bow wow," said Momma, "You are a good Puppy Dog." Then Momma Dog and Little Puppy Dog ran into the woods, and played and barked and had a lot of fun.

What do you think of that, Bud? Did Momma like the story?

Good night, love and kisses,

Sparky

Aug. 10, 1944

Dear Bud –

Did I ever tell you about the two goats we have here? One morning, we were awakened by sounds like a baby crying. "Me-he-he-he-haaaa." We looked outside, and there stood Billy Goat, black with white spots. He was eating our flowers. After every bite, he licked his nose and said, "Me-heh-hah-heh." We hollered at him and told him not to eat only our flowers. I guess he was a bad Billy goat because when we told him to stop, he went to the next hut and began to chew a shirt that was hanging on the clothesline.

We chased him away, but the next night there was twice as much "Me-heh-heh-heh-ing." We looked outside and we saw that Billy Goat had brought his wife along to enjoy the tasty flowers! Mrs. Billy Goat was a nanny goat. Her fur was the color of coffee, and she too had white spots. So Mr. and Mrs. Billy Goat ate, and ate, and after every few bites they looked at us and said, "Me-heh-heh-heh-hah-heh-a-a-a" and they looked at each other and ate more flowers. They ran all over the place.

One day, they ran into the kitchen and began to eat the cabbage. The cook chased them and threw a lot of tin cans at them. It was getting to be a problem. What to do with these goats? Well today, a little boy and his momma came to the hospital and asked if we had seen two goats. They were glad to find their long-lost goats and took them away, and Mr. and Mrs. Billy Goat said goodbye: "Meh-heh-heh-hah-a-a-a."

Sparky

Sept. 30, 1944

Dear Bud –

Did I tell you about the black and white cow? She lives next to our place all day. She walks around and swishes her tail. I guess she doesn't like flies. Every time a fly sits on her she switches her long tail and brushes the fly off. That cow is smart - always has her tail with her, to use as a fly swatter. This cow doesn't have to work, just walks around and eats grass all day. I never see her play. All she does is eat grass. I guess she doesn't feel like playing after eating nothing but grass.

The farmer who owns her is afraid she'll get lost, so he makes her wear a bell. Around her neck every time the cow moves, the bell goes "Clank, clank, clank." She never gets angry because it makes so much noise. She knows that when she gets lost, all she has to do is shake her head. When she shakes her head, the bell rings, then the farmer can hear the bell and find the cow. I asked her what her name was, but all she said was "Moo, moooo." All cows talk the same way. I don't think "Moo mooo" is her real name, do you?

The farmer says she is a good cow and gives him lots of fresh milk for his children. He says his children are growing big and strong because they drink lots of fresh milk. Isn't that fine? Are you drinking your milk? It will make you big and strong. Daddy will be very happy to know, that you are growing big and strong. Tell Momma to write me how much you love your milk.

Tell Momma I love her and my big fine boy lots and lots.

Sparky

Oct. 6, 1944

Dear Bud –

I got your letter and was very glad you had such a fine birthday party. I bet you had lots of fun eating that cake. Mama can make delicious cake, can't she? Aunt Sue wrote me that you talked like a big boy on the phone. I'm very proud of my big boy, so I got you a Jeep. We got lots of them here. We call our best one Johnny. Johnny the Jeep is a good Jeep. He hardly makes any noise as he runs around from place to place. His driver likes him too. His driver takes good care of Johnny. Every day, he washes Johnny with cold water, and Johnny just stands there and doesn't say a thing.

The only time Johnny talks is when his driver wants people to get out of the way. Then he presses Johnny on the horn. And Johnny says "Peep peep, here's a Jeep." And then the people get out of the way because they don't want Johnny the Jeep to run over them. The only thing that Johnny eats is gasoline. People don't like to eat gasoline, but Johnny is a Jeep. And that's the only thing that keeps a Jeep in good shape. They feed him with a big hose because Johnny has no hands. All he's got to move around with are wheels. You should hear Johnny drink his gasoline. "Gurgle gurgle" is what he says. Isn't that a funny way to eat your supper?

Johnny is very particular about his eyes. He has electric lights for eyes, and when he is out at night, he can see pretty far. I think Johnny likes little boys because he is so little himself. Aren't you glad you got a Jeep?

You are a good boy, and Daddy loves you.

Sparky

Oct. 22, 1944

Dear Bud –

Did I ever tell you about Danny? Danny is a donkey. He's got long ears and he can hear very well. He's got short legs, but they're very strong. Danny is used to working very hard every day. The farmer would hitch him to a cart. Then he would say "Giddyap" to Danny, and then Danny would begin to pull the cart up and down the hilly streets. The farmer used to load the cart with lots of bottles of milk. It was very heavy, and Danny would get angry sometimes and would just stand and rest and would not move. The farmer would shout and shout at Danny to make him move.

One day, Danny the Donkey got out of the pasture when the gate was unlocked. He thought he would run away and never work again. So Danny walked all over the hills without his cart. But soon he began to get hungry and could not find any grass he liked to eat. Then it began to rain, and Danny got cold and wet because he had no barn to stay in. Just then, the farmer found him – he missed Danny! "Such a fine donkey Danny is," he said. "Maybe I make him work too hard?"

So Danny was taken home. He ate and ate, and was so happy and warm in his nice, clean barn. And the farmer was so glad he never made Danny pull more than he should.

Wasn't that fine? Did you like the story Bud?

Good night,

Sparky

Nov. 7, 1944

Dear Bud –

Remember Danny the Donkey? Well, the farmer has a dog too. He is a bulldog. He is all white with big, round black spots on all parts of his body and face. That's why everyone calls him "Buttons," because it looks like he has big black buttons sewn onto his white fur coat.

Buttons is old, and he likes to snooze all curled up by the fireside. But no matter how soundly he is sleeping, he seems to hear well. At the slightest noise, he wakes up and growls, "Grr grr." He looks very fierce and ugly, but he is a good old dog. Even when he is happy, he growls because that is the only way he can talk. He likes to chew on bones. "Crunch, crunch, crunch." He chews and chews. Then he gets tired and falls asleep.

When the children want him to play, they try to take away Buttons' bones. Then Buttons wakes up fast and growls, "Grr, grr." He likes the children, and runs about and huffs and puffs. He likes to run after anything they throw and bring it back, puts it down on the ground. Buttons also likes to lick the children's faces when they bring him a bone to chew on, but the thing Buttons likes best of all is to lie curled up by the fireside and snooze and snooze.

What do you think of Buttons, Bud?

Sparky

Nov. 20, 1944

Dear Bud –

Did I ever tell you about Barney? Barney is our old broom. When we came here, he was given to us. They said he was a good broom and that he'd work fine if we treated him well. He is so nice and tall. All day long, he stands quietly in the corner. Funny thing though, he stands on his whiskers! Those whiskers are made of straw.

When Barney was new, his whiskers were nice and clean and straight. But every day we'd push his whiskers around the room and sweep up. Now, Barney's whiskers are very dirty, because every day he pushes dirt around with those whiskers. When Barney was new, he used to sing "Sweep, Sweep" when we pushed him along the floor. He was happy because he was so nice and clean. Now, Barney looks very sad standing there in the corner. He's sad because his whiskers are all twisted and dirty. He cries "Swoosh swoosh" when we try to sweep the room with him now. I guess he doesn't like to be dirty.

We're going to make Barney happy. I spoke to the man who puts new whiskers on old brooms. He promised to fix Barney and put nice clean whiskers on Barney again, pretty soon, Barney will be happy and proud. He'll have whiskers so nice and clean and straight. And, then, when we push him along the floor again, he will sing again, "Sweep, sweep, sweep."

Isn't that swell, Bud?

Daddy

Nov. 28, 1944

Dear Bud –

Did I ever tell you about Russell? Russell lives on the farm near us. He wakes up early every morning. The first thing he says is "Cock-a-doodle-doo!" He looks at the sun coming up and hollers it at it, "Cock-a-doodle-doo!" You are right, Bud. Russell is a rooster. He walks around bobbing his head and growls at the chickens, "Bit bit." They get out of his way because he makes so much noise. That's all he is good for is to make noise. He eats and struts and makes noise.

I asked the farmer why he keeps Russell. He told me that Russell is the best alarm clock in the world. Every morning, Russell wakes him up shouting, "Cock-a-doodle-doo." Russell is always so proud of being clean, he struts and shows off his fine brown feathers. And whenever anyone comes into the barnyard, Russell is there saying, "Bits kit cuddle." I guess he really is friendly and is just saying "Hello."

Russell the Rooster makes a lot of noise and some people don't like him, but the farmer says Russell is a good alarm clock, and he likes Russell. So I guess Russell must be a good rooster if someone likes him.

What do you think about it, Bud?

Sparky

Dec. 2, 1944

Dear Bud –

Snuffy is a snowman. He looks very funny because he is so round and white. The farmer's children made him out of snow. His eyes are made of pieces of coal, and they put a pipe in his mouth. The children sang and danced around Snuffy, but he didn't talk, just stood there and looked cold. Buttons the Bulldog growled at Snuffy. Buttons growls at everyone. Guess Buttons wanted the children to sing and dance around him. Then, Russell the Rooster jumped up on Snuffy the Snowman's head. Russell stuck out his head and said, "Cock-a-doodle-doo." But Snuffy just stood there and said nothing. Danny the Donkey came up and licked Snuffy's face. It must have tasted good because he licked and licked until the children chased him away.

Poor Snuffy just has to stay there out in the cold. Can't go anywhere because he is made of snow. Yesterday, Snuffy got very thin, the sun came out and shined on Snuffy, and he began to melt away. But the children got more snow and filled up Snuffy's head and belly. Now Snuffy is round and white as ever, but he can't talk, he just stands there and looks cold. I guess Snuffy is happy that way.

What do you think, Bud?

Sparky

Dec. 19, 1944

Dear Bud -

I just filled Stevie up with coal. Yep, Stevie is our new stove. He keeps us nice and warm. We just got him last week. He was all rusty and dirty, but we had him dressed up in a nice coat of black paint. Now he stands right in the middle of our hut. Haven't seen him sit down yet, but I suppose even a stove gets tired of standing.

You should hear Stevie roar when we throw coal into his mouth. That's what he likes most. Of course, he usually starts eating a few pieces of paper and wood - he knows that's good for stoves. But such roaring when he gets some delicious coal! Stoves are funny that way. They eat the wrong things. I guess that's why they get so hot with all that hot stuff burning up inside of them. Stevie has a big pipe stuck in his head. He's just like your daddy, smokes all the time and likes it when people are feeding him and making a fuss over him.

We take good care of Stevie every morning. He's cold because he's full of ashes. We clean him out and brush him off. He looks fine when he is clean and brushed. Yep, we take good care of Stevie now because he keeps us warm, but Stevie knows when summer comes we'll stop feeding him and forget about him. Yep, Stevie knows people only take care of things as long as they are needed. Stevie roared when I said that. Yep, Stevie is a good stove.

Good night Bud,

Daddy

Jan. 9, 1945

Dear Bud –

Do you know what Danny the Donkey did today? He walked over from that farm and came to our place. It was cold and snow was on the ground, but Danny was nice and warm because he has a fur coat on him all the time. I didn't know Danny was near our place, but the farmer said Danny must be here -- Danny left his nice warm barn and walked over here.

I looked on the ground and sure enough, there we saw Danny's hoofs had made marks in the snow. So, I went with the farmer to help him find Danny. We followed the marks Danny had made in the snow. Guess Danny likes to look around at night. Every hut had his hoof marks by the door. On and on we followed the hoof marks. Then we heard "Crunch, crunch" by the mess hall. There was Danny the Donkey! Guess what he was doing? He was eating carrots. Beautiful fresh carrots! "Crunch, crunch" and Danny ate another carrot. Danny must love carrots because he walked far in the cold and snow to eat his carrots. "Crunch, crunch" — that's the lovely sound carrots make when Danny eats them.

Isn't that swell Bud?

Sparky

Jan. 18, 1945

Dear Bud —

Did I tell you about Charlie? I'm sitting on him now, so he can't see what I'm writing. That's right, you guessed it, Charlie is a chair. He has four legs. They're very strong legs, but he never walks. Wherever we put him, he stands. He stands day and night in the same spot. He never says anything, just stands there waiting for someone to sit on him. I guess he doesn't like to be sat upon either. Every time someone sits on him, he squeaks and creaks: "Creak squeak CREAK!" Then he just keeps quiet until he feels you moving around in his lap. And there he grunts, "Hemmp, hurrmp." I don't know what that means. Do you? Maybe it means you're too heavy?

Oh yes, Charlie is pretty strong. His arms are very thick and hard. Charlie's arms help him hold you on his lap. Charlie has a nice soft lap. He is very nice to sit on. I'd like to sit on him when I write you letters. Charlie creaked just now. I guess he knows you are a fine boy. I know he'd love to have you sit on his lap sometimes.

I think Charlie gets angry with me, especially when I tried to stand on him. Now that is one thing a good chair like Charlie does not like. When I stand on his arms he groans, "Aaah aaah," and when I stand in his lap he squeals, "Eeeee." I guess Charlie the Chair only likes people to sit in his lap!

What do you think of that Bud?

Sparky

Jan. 21, 1945

Dear Bud –

Everyone slept late today. But it all was because Russell didn't wake us up. You remember Russell? Russell the Rooster. Every morning he gets up when the sun gets up. He sits on the fence and hollers at the sun. He says, "Cock-a-doodle-doo." But the sun says nothing and keeps on shining. But this morning we didn't hear Russell. And when Russell doesn't holler, we just sleep. Do you know why Russell didn't holler today? I went over to find out. It was very cold last night, and Russell was cold too. So he jumped into the cellar to get warm. But he couldn't get out. So he decided to just stay there and keep warm. Russell loves to be nice and warm. I went down into the cellar, and Russell said, "Kit cut kit" and ran around in circles.

Russell didn't want to get out of that nice warm cellar. But we have to get up for work every morning, so Russell had to come out and work too. Tomorrow morning Russell will sit on the fence and holler, "Cock-a-doodle-doo" and everyone will get up.

Ok, Bud?

Sparky

Jan. 28, 1945

Dear Bud –

When I went outdoors today, I found lots of snow all over the place. I knew it would be a fine time to go up the hill to the farmhouse, so I walked up there through the snow, and I wish you were here because it was such fun. When I got to the farm house I saw Snuffy. Yes, our old friend Snuffy the Snowman!

He stood there, smiling nice and white. My, he felt so cold when I touched him. But Snuffy is made of snow and he never minds the cold. The farmer's children were having a jolly time. They were dancing and singing in a circle, and Snuffy stood there in the center and just smiled and said nothing. I guess Snuffy likes to hear children sing and see them so jolly. They sang: "Snuffy don't walk; Snuffy, don't talk. Snuffy is all snow, oh-oh-ohhhhh!" And Snuffy just stood there and said nothing, and just smiled and smiled. Again and again, they danced in a circle. And sang and sang. My, they had a jolly time with Snuffy the Snowman! Such happy children!

Don't you think so, Bud?

Sparky

Feb. 4, 1945

Dear Bud –

There was a lot of noise over the farmer's house today. We could hear it all the way down here. Russell the Rooster was shouting "Cock-a-doodle-doo" at the top of his voice. I wondered what was going on, so I went up to see. When I got to the farmyard there was Danny the Donkey, hollering "Hee haw haw." And stamping his feet up and down. Of course, Russell was keeping up his Cock-a-doodle-doo too, and Buttons the Bulldog was growling, "Grr-grr-grr."

It wasn't too cold, so I knew they weren't freezing. They were standing by the barn and making so much noise! I looked into see what was the matter. Well, all the nice straw from Danny's bed was out in a pile, and Russell's nest was also mixed up. Buttons doesn't live in the barn, but I guess he was growling because the others were noisy. I asked the farmer what was going on. He said, "I'm just making up some fresh beds for them." And he did! And Danny and Russell and Buttons made no more noise. I guess they were happy to have their straw beds fresh and clean.

Is that right Bud?

Sparky

Feb. 8, 1945

Dear Bud –

Gee that Danny gets into some funny places. Remember Danny the Donkey? Well, he was standing around the barnyard with nothing to do but eat his hay. Donkeys eat hay, instead of nice cereal because they can't hold a spoon in their hoofs, I guess. Anyhow, Danny was quietly munching his hay, "Cirrunch, crunch, Cirrrunch" — just like that. Then guess what the farmer brought to the kitchen? Carrots! Danny began to hop up and down, he was so happy. Nice, fresh, crisp carrots! Mmmm!

But the farmer and his family like carrots too, so they sat by the table eating their carrots and enjoying that beautiful sound which carrots make when you bite one: "Sklimpf-Sklumpf!" Danny came to the window and looked at them, eating those lovely carrots. Danny hung his tongue out and licked the window, but no one gave him a carrot. So, our Danny, being a wise donkey, just walked up the steps into the kitchen and grabbed a carrot in his mouth and ran out into the barn yard, and Danny the Donkey ate his carrot, "Crunch, crunch."

Smart, eh? Bud?

Sparky

Feb. 14, 1945

Dear Bud –

Your puppy dog brought Daddy that fine Valentine from you today. "Yip Yip, Bud loves his Daddy, " the puppy dog said, and Daddy was very happy because the puppy dog licked your daddy's nose. You know, Bud, how a nose tickles when it's licked? Well, the puppy dog jumped up and down. He was so happy to get out of that envelope.

He was hungry too! I got him a nice supper, and he drank lots of nice fresh milk. Then he ran around wagging his tail. I took him up to the farm house, and Buttons the Bulldog growled, "Grr, Grr," and was glad to have the puppy dog stay with him. Your puppy dog now has a nice warm home. Are you glad, Bud? I am.

Kiss Momma,

Sparky

Feb. 18, 1945

Dear Bud –

My, what a lovely day it was today. Your old daddy sure wished his boy was here. The sky was very blue, and the clouds are nice and fluffy just like vanilla ice cream. Yep, Bud, your old daddy took a nice walk in the country. The little birds were very happy and sang and flew from tree to tree. Did you ever see a bird fly, Bud? They fly just like airplanes, and never need any gasoline, and they sing prettily too. "Tweet twitter twitter tweet."

You would enjoy hearing the little bird with yellow feathers on his chest. He would puff out his chest until I thought he would burst and then he began to sing, "Tweet twitter tweet twitter." And another bird (I guess it was his wife?) would answer, "Twitter tweet twitter, tweet."

I tried hard, but I just couldn't guess what it all meant. Do you think they were talking of what a lovely day it was? I said to the birds that my Bud would love to hear them sing. And do you know what the birds answered? They said, "Tweet tweet tweet twitter twitter twitter!" And they sure sounded happy! I think they wanted me to tell you, Bud, that they'd love to sing for you. What do you think of Twitter and Tweet, your bird friends?

Good birds, eh, Bud?

Sparky

March 22, 1945

Dear Bud –

It was such a fine day today. Just outside my hut, on the big tree, sat Twitter and tweet singing. Remember them, Bud? Twitter and Tweet are little birds. They love to fly round & round. They fly very high, too. You should hear them flap their wings as they fly. They don't seem to get tired, either. Birds are funny that way. They can hardly walk without getting tired. Most of the time they hop when they try to walk, but when they want to go somewhere as quickly, all they have to do is spread their wings, flap flap & jump up into the air - and away they fly.

Twitter and Tweet like to sit high in the tree and sing. Did you ever hear birds sing? "Twitter twitter, tweet tweet," over and over again. And it sounds very lovely. Birds like to be out in the fresh air and sunshine. It makes them feel so happy and gay. I guess that's why they love to sing. "Tweet twitter, tweet twitter."

I wonder what that means, Bud? Maybe Twitter and Tweet are just saying that they are so happy - eh, Bud? Yes - it's very nice to be out in the fresh air and sunshine. It makes you strong and happy. Kiss Momma for me.

Good night, Bud.

Sparky

April 6, 1945

Dear Bud –

It was very hot today, so I decided to walk over to the farmer's house to get an ice cold glass of milk. My, doesn't milk taste swell when it's nice and cold?

I got to the farmer's house, but no one was there! I looked inside, and Buttons the Bulldog was gone. I went to the barn, and Russell the Rooster was gone. I looked in the orchard and Danny the Donkey was gone, too. Gosh, that seemed very queer! Not even the farmer or his children were around. I looked in the cornfield, but no one was there. I looked up into the trees, and Twitter and Tweet, our little birds, were also gone. "Tsk tsk, what can the matter be?" I thought.

So, I decided to take a walk to the little lake not far from here. As I came there, closer and closer, I began to hear splashing noises, and then I heard growling and birds singing and rooster crowing. Then I saw the lake. What a sight! On the edge of the water stood Buttons the Bulldog. He said hello to me: "Grr grr." And Twitter and Tweet were flying around, tweeting and twittering. And Russell the Rooster was hopping up and down, hollering, "Cock-a-doodle-doo."

And in the water, guess what I saw? Danny the Donkey! "Gee, he was having fun! He swam back and forth, and such splashing! And he laughed, "Hee Haw." I guess. Danny the Donkey just loves to swim. Swimming makes him healthy and strong.

Good night, Bud,

Sparky

April 21, 1945

Dear Bud –

It was such a lovely day today, the sun was nice and warm. I was going to take a snooze on my bunk, but I thought it would be nicer to sleep on the grass. So, I took my blanket and went out into the pasture. I found a very tall tree with big branches, covered up with lots and lots of green leaves. I spread my blanket in the shade of that tree. I went to sleep, but soon I was awakened by something licking my nose. It was our friend Buttons the Bulldog. "Go away and let me sleep!" I said, and Buttons went away.

I fell asleep again, and soon I was awakened by something pecking at my nose. It was our friend Russell the Rooster. "Go away and let me sleep!" I said, and Russell went away. I fell asleep again, and soon I was awakened by some things hopping on my head. It was our friends Twitter and Tweet the little birds. "Go away and let me sleep!" I said, and Twitter and tweet went away.

I fell asleep again and soon I was awakened by something pulling my tie. It was our old friend Danny the Donkey. "Go away and let me sleep," I said. But Danny just stayed there and pulled my tie. Donkeys are stubborn, I guess. So, I folded up my blanket and walked back to my hut and got on my bunk and fell asleep. It's good to sleep in my own bunk.

Good night, Bud,

Sparky

May 6, 1945

Dear Bud –

Gee, I was hungry! I was coming home from a long walk, and I wanted to eat. So, I stopped by the farmhouse. Buttons the Bulldog looked at me and ran out into the yard. He dug up a big bone and brought it to me. "Buttons," I said, "I can't eat bones!" So, Buttons growled, "Grr grr" and sat down and chewed up his bone and smacked his chops. That's the way Button says, "Yum yum!"

Then Twitter and Tweet flew by and dropped a nice fat worm in front of me. "Twitter and Tweet," I said. "I can't eat worms." So, Twitter and Tweet sat down and ate up the worm and said, "Twitter" and "Tweet." That's the way Twitter and Tweet say "Yum yum!" Then Russell the Rooster brought me a pile of corn kernels. "Russell," I said. "I can't eat corn kernels raw." So Russell sat down and ate the corn kernels raw and said, "Cock-a-doodle-doo!" That's the way Russell says "Yum-yum."

Then Johnny the Jeep rode up and brought me a can of gasoline! "Johnny," I said. 'I can't drink gasoline!" So, Johnny drank the gasoline and said, "Gurgle glug gurgle." That's the way Johnny says "Yum yum!"

Then Danny the Donkey brought me some nice fresh hay. "Danny, I said. "I can't eat hay!" So, Danny the Donkey ate up all the hay and said, "Munch crunch munch." That's the way Danny says "Yum yum!"

So, I was still hungry, Bud, when I got back to camp. But in the mess hall was some nice, cold milk! "Oh hooray," I said. "I sure can drink milk." So I drank the milk and I said, "Yum, yum" because I love milk, and that's how I say "Yum yum!"

Good night, Bud!

Sparky

June 7, 1945

Dear Bud –

Gee, it's been a long time since I wrote you a letter, Bud. Well, it's because I've been away travelling. You know how a fellow gets tired and sleepy from riding trains, don't you, Bud? I saw lots and lots of things, Bud, as my train ran through the fields.

There were black and white cows, and brown and white cows. And everywhere these cows went, they were followed by calves who were always hungry. You know that a cow is a calf's momma, and there were too many sheep to count. Their wool was not very white, it's because the sheep here over here sleep on the ground.

Tell me, Bud, do the sheep back home sleep in beds? They must, because their wool seems much whiter. Everywhere I saw sheep. There were also lots of lambs. They all looked the same, but do you know that each momma sheep always could pick out her own lamb. I wonder how they do it?

Then I saw the ocean splashing all over the rocks. Never gets tired, that ocean, splashing and roaring and making a fuss all the time. Wonder if the ocean is upset because it's wet all day and night?

Yes, but I saw lots of things while I rode on those trains. and you should see the trains! They're smaller than ours and make more smoke and dirt. They'll be better when they grow up- eh, Bud?

Good night,

Sparky

June 16, 1945

Dear Bud –

Did I ever tell you about the big hill I climbed last week? It's been here all the time, but it looked so high I never thought I'd go up there. Well, Bud, it was a tough job. The sheep run up and down the hill with no trouble at all, and not once did I see a sheep slip or fall, but sheep got four feet and people only have two feet. Maybe that's why sheep can stand way up there. They jump from rock to rock. And they don't wear shoes, either. They holler all the time, though, and all the time they're saying, "Baaah." I don't know whether they holler because their feet hurt, or because they never learn to talk better. Well, Bud, I climbed up that hill all right, and as I got higher and higher, all the houses down below looked smaller and smaller, and big trains looked like little choo-choos, and big trucks looked like teeny toys and people looked like little specks of dust just creeping along.

I felt pretty big up there, but then I saw more sheep and they were climbing higher and higher, and all the time they were hollering "Baaaah." I guess sheep will always run around barefoot, and they always holler no matter how high they climb. And I was very glad I wasn't a sheep with nothing to eat but grass, and nothing to say but "Baaah," even though they can climb pretty high and fast.

Good night, Bud,

Sparky

ABOUT ISADORE "SPARKY" SPARK

Isadore "Sparky" Spark (1909-2005) was a lifelong storyteller and punster who would greet his grandkids with the question: "Would you like to comp my keepany?" Sparky was born in Philadelphia to a family in the fish business, but a severe childhood illness inspired him to study medicine and become a doctor. He joined the Army Medical Corps and trained in neurology and psychiatry.

After the outbreak of WWII, Sparky was sent overseas to the 55th General Hospital based in England and later France. Among his many responsibilities was to treat shell-shocked (PTSD) patients. He was well suited to this task, as his demeanor was warm, friendly and sympathetic. After the war, he was promoted to the rank of Lt. Colonel, discharged from the Army, and practiced as a psychoanalyst for many years.

Sparky married Geraldine Milgram in 1940 and they had three children, Ronald, Michelle and Daniel, and two puppy dogs, Queenie I and II.

Michelle Seigei Spark is an artist and art therapist who lives in Phoenicia, New York, and Ronald Spark, M.D. is a retired pathologist who lives in Tucson, Arizona.

Book cover and interior design by Diana Kado

Made in the USA
Coppell, TX
17 March 2026

74133909R00028